The Last Church!

Are you caught in its web of deception?

By Pastor Thomas A. Robb

The Last Church
Copyright © 2007 by Thomas Robb

Watch the Sunday morning church service of the Christian Revival Center with Pastor Thomas Robb

Live video stream.
12 noon Eastern
11:00 am Central
10:00 am Mountain
9:00 am Pacific
www.ChristianRevivalCenter.net

Christian Revival Center
PO Box 602
Harrison, AR 72602

Did you know . . .
The anti-Christ is a
Christian?

Surprised! Most people wouldn't even give it a thought. After all, for years we have been told the anti-Christ will be some evil person. He is pictured as a cross between a grotesque beast and an evil genius, forcing people to worship him instead of Jesus.

Some have even developed elaborate stories of how this anti-Christ will give Christians an opportunity to publicly reject Jesus and if they don't, they will be instantly arrested or possibly killed. According to their story, armed soldiers of the anti-Christ will march into churches, rip Bibles away from the hands of worshipers and force them to publicly deny Jesus Christ.

But is this really what will happen or is it just a fairy tale, the product of an overactive imagination? In fact, is it possible that this anti-Christ won't appear evil at all? Is it possible that the anti-Christ will appear as a Christian - a devoted follower of Jesus Christ?

Stop and consider, the Bible tells us that this anti-Christ will deceive many (Matthew 24, Revelation. 20). We are also told that the people will "worship" (love) him, Revelation 13.

Keep in mind that the great battle of the ages is between Jesus Christ and Lucifer. We read in Isaiah 14 that Satan organized a rebellion against God. Most preachers will point out this passage and tell us that Satan wants to be like God and have people worship him. While this is partially true, there is something else going on here that most preachers miss. Satan is not simply seeking vain worship but instead, it is his intention of becoming the great universal *law giver*.

To do so, he must change the law given by God. Christian people understand that in the last days we will enter a time when because of wickedness, man will be confused and unable to identify the difference

Between good and evil. This is brought upon us because the last church has become weak and tolerant. The Bible says it is neither cold or hot (Revelations 3:14 -15). Unfortunately, the vast overwhelming majority of Christians have themselves become a victim of the very thing of which they attempt to warn others. A good example of this is seen in how the issue of homosexuality is treated. Up until not too many years ago, it was understood that homosexuals had a mental disorder. However, with the change of our culture, all this has been altered and now homosexuals are presented as normal people who simply have a different kind of love. Those who refuse to accept their *"different kind of love"* are looked upon as homophobic - a mental disorder!

Another example is seen in the post-Christian churches attitude towards interracial marriage. For years the Christian Church did not accept race-mixing, however, today an evil spirit has arisen in the church that not only permits interracial marriage but actually suggests that those who oppose interracial marriage are sinners.
Let me give an example of an incident which happened with a young White Christian couple from Texas. They were attending a nice all-White Baptist church in the Dallas/Ft. Worth area. One Sunday morning, their little old girl was told by her Sunday school teacher that if she did not go and play with the new black boy who came to church she was making Jesus unhappy and He might not let her go to heaven.

Naturally, the little girl was traumatized.

These as well as other cancerous attacks upon our faith have neutralized and weakened the church and have created a new Christianity and a new Jesus Christ.

This NEW Jesus is tolerant of homosexuality and as for interracial marriage; this New Age Jesus not only tolerates interracial marriage but actually embraces it.

Christians who are following the new teachings of the church have become totally caught up in the doctrine of tolerance.

In fact, we are being told that one of the greatest attributes of Jesus Christ is his tolerance! But the truth is just the opposite. Jesus Christ is the God of *intolerance.*

TOLERANCE IS AN ACT OF SATANIC WORSHIP

Satan is the god of tolerance! It doesn't matter what kind of moral standard you have or don't have. You can be an atheist or a Sunday church going "Christian," you can be straight or you can be "gay," you can have high morals, low morals or no morals, you can be a preacher or you can be a pornographer, you can be a drunkard, a dope dealer, a Sunday School teacher or a pedophile. To each of you, Satan has his arms wide open - he loves you all and you are all welcome into the great One World Church of Satan.

Yes . . . *EVERYONE!*

But Jesus is the God of intolerance. He said the road to eternal life is a narrow road and a straight gate, (Matthew 7). There are absolutes of right and wrong and He does not tolerate those who choose wrong.

The Church of Satan, however, is not called the Church of Satan. It is the great One World Church of Mystery Babylon, preaching in the name of Jesus and deceiving many (Matthew 24:5,11; Mark 13:6).

2 Thessalonians 2:3 tells us that prior to the return of Christ there would come a *"great falling away."* Some preachers claim this is referring to a rapture. However, the meaning is clear. There will come a falling away from the Gospel. The Darby Translation gives the meaning to be *"a great apostasy."* This *"falling away"* (apostasy) is a reference to Christian people who are weak and cannot stand as a faithful servant. They are the ones who according to Revelation 3:14 are *"neither cold nor hot."* They are weak, cowardly Christians without a backbone and thus fall from the faith!

It is through these weak Christians that the great One World Church will rise. They do not have the courage to resist the satanic doctrines of interracial marriage and homosexuality. They do not have the backbone to protect their Christian heritage from the flood of aliens coming into our midst. They do not have the spiritual understanding needed to establish Christian dominion in the earth. It appears that their whole intent is to prove over and over again how loving and tolerant they are.

And from this One World Church a new Jesus is emerging. And the new Christians of this new church are taking the new doctrine of brotherhood and tolerance to the world. They are marching in the name of their new Jesus, under their new flag, their new doctrines and their new faith. Gone is the "hatred" and "bigotry" of the old church.

BEHOLD! The great new "Christian" church!

Are we not told in scripture that there will be those who will claim they preached in the name of Jesus, but in Matthew 7:23 Jesus tells them, *"depart from me you workers of iniquity."*

> *"Not every one that saith unto me, Lord, Lord, shall enter into the kingdom of heaven; but he that doeth the will of my Father which is in heaven. Many will say to me in that day, Lord, Lord, have we not prophesied in thy name? and in thy name have cast out devils? and in thy name done many wonderful works? And then will I profess unto them, I never knew you: depart from me, ye that work iniquity."*
>
> Matt 7:21-23

The word iniquity is from the Greek word *ajnomiva* and is pronounced Anomia in the English and it means lawlessness and has been translated as such in other translations. Here is the way the New King James Bible translates the last verse of this passage.

> *"And then I will declare to them, 'I never knew you; depart from Me, you who practice lawlessness!"*

The *Darby Translation* is similar,

> *"And then will I avow unto them, I never knew you. Depart from me, workers of lawlessness."*

I want you to understand that these were not preachers who violated man's law, they were not even guilty of violating ecclesiastical law, but they were violators of the law of God. They have joined the rebellion!

We can look at all kinds of religious laws. Many, if not most of these "laws" are silly. Even the "religious" laws (rituals) found in the Old Testament (which was the "door" to God) are silly. Am I being sacrilegious when I say the religious laws of the Old Testament were silly? I don't think so!

Why can I say that?

It is evident that even God thought the religious laws (rituals) of the old covenant were silly, that is why they were nailed to the Cross and replaced with the blood of Jesus, the Lamb of God.

They were silly because with the sacrifice of Christ on the Cross, He became the "door." Jesus tells us in John 10:9, *"I am the door: by me if any man enter in, he shall be saved."* Jesus is the ONLY door by which a person can have peace with the Father. Any other approach or attempt is foolish.

So we read in Scripture (Matthew 7) that the Day of Judgment would come upon us and there would be many standing in the presence of God proclaiming their dedication, their loyalty and their love for Jesus. But it is recorded that Jesus tells them to depart from His presence because, in spite of their profession of love, they were workers of iniquity (lawlessness).

These workers of iniquity are not simply guilty of preaching a mild, liberal form of Christianity, but were actually corrupters of *natural* law and were guilty of preaching a doctrine of tolerance towards race mixing and homosexuality.

Why do I say that? Keep reading and you will understand!

These workers of iniquity are ushering in the great ONE WORLD CHURCH. It is a multiracial church rising in defiance to the true and faithful church of God.

If Christians want to discover where they can find the spirit of anti-Christ, they should not look for some evil dictator. They need to look no further than their local Christian minister proclaiming the gospel of tolerance and racial reconciliation.

You must be wise enough to know that this One World Church of Mystery Babylon is a "Christian" church but also wise enough to know that it is an APOSTATE Christian Church!

> *"Many will say to me in that day, 'Lord, Lord, have we not prophesied in thy name? and in thy name have cast out devils? and in thy name done many wonderful works?' And then will I profess unto them, I never knew you: depart from me, ye that work iniquity."*
>
> Matthew 7:22-23

FALSE SHEPHERDS

There is little doubt that the vast majority of Christians are totally unaware of the enormous complexity of the satanic rebellion which has targeted them.

The Judeo-Christian church has confused many, if not most Christians, and has led them to focus on a Satan who goes about tempting us to be "naughty." The sin which Satan is tempting us to commit will vary according to the teaching of a church, denomination or preacher. For some, these sins will include smoking, drinking or gambling. To others it will perhaps be drinking coffee, watching TV or women wearing shorts, pants or lipstick. For an increasing number of those in the Judeo-Christian (post-Christian) church it is intolerance and bigotry.

in the Church ●

However, the Apostle Paul (Ephesians 6:12) is clear that the intrigue of the satanic rebellion, which we can read about in Isaiah 14, is massive and much more powerful than the understanding of many who think a personal encounter with Satan tempted them to sin.

I am aware that this may go against orthodoxy; However, I believe the Scriptures show that sins which we commit are not because of the temptation of Satan but rather because of our sinful nature and carnal lusts.

In other words, Satan is not tempting you, so don't blame Satan for your sin. You sin because it is your *nature* to sin! You sin because *you chose to do so!*

So if Satan is not tempting you to sin, then what is he doing? Paul says in Ephesians 6:12,

> *"For we wrestle not against flesh and blood, but against principalities, against powers, against the rulers of the darkness of this world, against spiritual wickedness in high places."*

While preacher after preacher after preacher is going about warning their "flock" to be careful because Satan is sneaking up on them, our nation continues its spiral flush down the proverbial toilet.

Paul gives warning that there is arraigned against us "principalities", "powers", and "spiritual wickedness" and these things are found in "high places."

There is the concerted effort to rot out our nation, rob us of our faith, corrupt our children, deny us our birthright, undermine our racial heritage, impoverish our people, deny us our wages, exploit our compassion, pollute our minds, demoralize our youth, make us shameful of our accomplishments and to hate our forefathers. And instead of warning our people, the ministers of God, which we have appointed over us, say nothing except "love Jesus!" It is like a disobedient child who will throughout the day deliberately disobey the instructions of his mother and then at the end of the day says, *"I love you mommy!"*

God - is not so easily manipulated!

There is the concerted effort to rot out our nation, rob us of our faith, corrupt our children, deny us our birthright, undermine our racial heritage, impoverish our people, deny us our wages, exploit our compassion, pollute our minds, demoralize our youth, make us shameful of our accomplishments and to hate our forefathers. And instead of warning our people, the ministers of God, which we have appointed over us, say nothing!

WHO IS TO BLAME?

The question is not easily answered because we could point the finger at many. However, it seems that the Bible lays much of the blame on preachers. In

7

other words, as disturbing as it may be for some to hear, the fact is that the great burden of sin which is upon the nation is not the fault of the pool halls, the cigarette companies, the breweries, the movie industry or any one of a number of things toward which we are prone to point. The sin of the nation is found behind the pulpits of our churches!

I do not know of any place in Scripture where God tells the pool halls to sound a warning to the nation. I do not know of any place where God tells cigarette companies, *"Go forth and tell my people to repent."* I think you could search the Scriptures the rest of your life and no where will you ever find God sending forth the media with the mission to proclaim the Gospel.

And you know why he didn't tell them to preach a message of repentance? Because it isn't their job! It is the preachers who are called to give warning to the nation and the preachers have been a miserable failure.

The ministers of God are to warn the nation of impending disaster. Not just personal sin, but national disaster brought about by our national sin.

Let us look at two scriptures that reveal the responsibility of God's servants.

> *"Cry aloud, spare not, lift up thy voice like a trumpet, and shew my people their transgression, and the house of Jacob their sins"*
> Isaiah 58:1

> *"Son of man, I have made thee a watchman unto the house of Israel: therefore hear the word at my mouth, and give them warning from me."*
> Ezekiel 3:17

Today our nation is in chaos. Illegal aliens flood our nation to steal our inheritance. Homosexuals are knocking down the door of our moral sensitivities. Our Christian foundation is being eaten away by the termites of Secular Humanism. Our children are being corrupted by the occult teachings of racial brotherhood. The unborn are being sacrificed to please the gods of abortion. Our national leaders are undermining the sovereignty of America. Our public schools are tools of progressive education and our churches are becoming the gateway to the One World Church.

And in the midst of all this, the vast majority of our preachers do and say nothing!

Oh! They will wail and they will toss and turn as if they are in great pain over the condition of our nation. But they will not allow their lifestyle to be disturbed or their standing in the community to be in jeopardy.

If you think I am being too harsh, read what God says in Isaiah 56:10-11,

> "His watchmen are blind: they are all ignorant, they are all dumb dogs, they cannot bark; sleeping, lying down, loving to slumber. Yea, they are greedy dogs which can never have enough, and they are shepherds that cannot understand: they all look to their own way, every one for his gain, from his quarter."

Many preachers wail and cry about how our nation has become sinful but then say, *"Oh well, the Bible says in the last days sin will abound and it will get worse and worse . . . Nothing we can do about it. . . Pass the collection plate!"*

DEPART from me

"Beware of false prophets, which come to you in sheep's clothing, but inwardly they are ravening wolves. Ye shall know them by their fruits . . . Not everyone that saith unto me, Lord, Lord shall enter into

Sometimes you will hear preachers speak out about our sin nature, but most of the time we are just told that if you are unhappy, if your life is not working out too well, if you are having a bad marriage or your kids are driving you up the wall, then you can find a better life by loving Jesus and turning your life over to Him.

That's it! If you will only love Jesus then you will have a happy life and go to heaven.

They fail to understand the key word of the Gospel - repent!

I must be careful because I am aware that it may appear that I am making light of the cleansing power of the blood of Jesus. However, it is not the power of the blood which I am attempting to examine, but it is the lives of those who claim to love Jesus, but who are in reality promoting a New Age form of Christianity.

Keep in mind, such people DO exist and the Bible warns us of their existence. Jesus said they will claim to love Him and will have done many great and wonderful things in the name of Jesus. However, in reality they promote iniquity and lawlessness!

The Greek word for iniquity is ajnomiva (anomia) and it means wickedness, unrighteousness and violation of the law. This cannot mean violators of man's law, but could only be correctly understood to be violators of God's law and would have reference to those who are in rebellion to God's law and authority.

But what sin would put us in rebellion against God? The Bible tells us in Romans 3:23, "For all have sinned and come short of the glory of God."

10

I think the Bible is clear; we are all sinners and sin because of our nature. However, being a sinner does not make you a part of this rebellion against God and His authority, especially for those who have had a regeneration of their heart. It is not being a sinner that makes you part of the rebellion but your willingness to tolerate or actively promote the changing of God's law.

Keep in mind there is a rebellion. Isaiah 14 tells us of this satanic rebellion which has been in existence from the beginning of time.

While we look at those who, in this final hour, profess to be servants of God and have done mighty works in the name of Jesus, it is interesting to note that when they are rejected they protest, claiming to be servants of God and begin to name the mighty works they have performed in the name of Jesus.

> *"Many will say to me in that day, 'Lord, Lord, have we not prophesied in thy name? and in thy name have cast out devils? and in thy name done many wonderful works?'*

In other words, they REALLY BELIEVED and thought they were being faithful! However, even in their profession of faith they were engaged in a great sin. The kind of sin which the Judeo-Christian church tolerates - but God does not!

Please understand.

1) These false ministers really believe they were servants of God.

2) They did many mighty works in the name of Jesus.

3) They professed to love Jesus.

4) However, they were violators of the law.

5) The law they violated could not have been man's law because man's law is not divine and can not condemn man to "hell."

6) All people sin (Roman 3:23) so their conduct was something more than the sin which all people have.

7) The sin in which they were engaged had to be something other than the sin which we all have.

8) Their sin was actually a challenge to the authority of God. In other words they promoted the rebellion!

THEIR SIN WAS THE SIN OF TOLERANCE!

I know this is not what your preachers are telling you. I know this is not what Kenneth Copeland, Jesse Duplantis, Jimmy Swaggart, Marcus Lamb, Joel Osteen, John Hagee, Ken Ham or any of the other

New Age preachers you could name will tell you. But tolerance is a SIN! It is an act of satanic worship! It is the foundation of the One World Church.

I know you have been told that a Christian is to display love and tolerance. In fact, to most people who are being led into the One World Church - Jesus Christ is the perfect example of tolerance.

But let us look at the scripture again! *"Enter ye in at the strait gate: for wide is the gate, and broad is the way, that leadeth to destruction, and many there be which go in thereat: Because strait is the gate, and narrow is the way, which leadeth unto life, and few there be that find it."* Matthew 7:14.

Here is the New Century Translation.

"But the gate is small and the road is narrow that leads to true life. Only a few people find that road."

Jesus Christ is telling us that the road to hell is a wide road and the road to life is a narrow road.

In other words there ARE absolutes. There are things which are right and things which are wrong regardless of what the date may be on the calendar.

IS ALL TOLERANCE BAD?

Of course not! However, there is a certain kind of tolerance that leads to hell and a certain kind of intolerance that leads to life.

But how can we know the difference?

The Sermon on the Mount was given to the disciples. It is a sermon of Christian brotherhood.

Christ is telling the *church* (His followers) that you are to love each other. There is to be no division. Does this mean that every one is going to be in agreement?

I don't think so. It would be nice if this was the case. But I think Jesus Christ is telling us that we are to love each other in spite of our disagreements.

Over the years Christian people have often fought against each other. If you worship on the "wrong" day, there will be someone telling you that you are not a "real" Christian. If you baptize "wrong," or if you do not baptize, then you are not a "real" Christian and cannot be a part of the true church. If you have music in your church, or the "wrong" kind of music with the "wrong" kind of instruments, you cannot be a "real" Christian and will probably go to hell. There are those who say you must pray in the name of Yahweh, the sacred name of God, or he will not answer your prayers. There is the Church of Christ, Methodist, Presbyterians, Baptist, Assemblies of God, Lutherans, etc. All divided over silly stuff.

Maybe you don't see it this way. I am simply telling you the way I see it.

In spite of all these divisions (and many more) Jesus is telling us to love one another. Be tolerant! Do you have long hair? Speak in tongues? Take communion in the right manner, allow the "right" kind of music? Do women wear make-up, wear pants? There are those who think the use of electricity is a terrible sin, or driving a car, etc. But as Christians we are to have tolerance to our Christian brothers and sisters who do not see the things the same way we see them. In other words we are to "love one another."

But there are TWO things of which we are not to tolerate. These two things are the foundation of the ONE WORLD CHURCH.

One of these sins is now almost fully accepted by the modern New Age Christian church. In other words almost all Christian churches have become tolerant of one of these two abominable sins.

The second of these two sins is still mildly opposed by most Christians; however, in time they will accept it and become tolerant of it also.

These two foundational pillars of the One World Church are becoming more and more acceptable by Christians.

I am Simply telling you the way I See it!

But what makes these false teachers guilty of having the wrong kind of tolerance - the going to hell kind of tolerance?

Race & Gender

Matthew 7:21-23 is a somewhat shocking scripture because it tells us that there will be preachers who preach in the name of Jesus, cast out demons in the name of Jesus and who did many wonderful works in the name of Jesus - yet - in spite of this devotion to Jesus Christ they are rejected by the very one they served. Jesus Christ says to them, *"Depart from me for I never knew you!"*

It is my opinion, and you may not see it the way I do, but I believe this scripture is speaking about preachers who are a part of the One World Church.

Even though the anti-Christ appears as a Christian, he is promoting a false Christianity. The Satanic rebellion intends to alter Christianity into a form which would be unrecognizable by the early church.

Remember these rejected preachers PREACHED Jesus Christ! They taught in His name and did many wonderful works. All this was done in the name of Jesus Christ.

What was their reward? They were rejected by Jesus! Why?

I believe it is safe to say that it was not because they violated some silly church "law." Also, I think it is safe to say it was not for violating some law of man.

It had to be more severe than simply being sinful, for we are ALL sinful. The Bible is clear we all commit sin! Without the covering of the blood atonement, even the most righteous among us is as a filthy rag to the Lord.

"But we are all as an unclean thing, and all our righteousness is as filthy rags." - Isaiah 64:6

It is apparent that they were guilty of something much more sinister than our sin nature.

Keep in mind that as recorded in Isaiah 14, Satan is in rebellion against God and brought his rebellion to the earth. When reading Isaiah 14, most preachers will tell us that Satan wants to be wor-

14

shipped like God is worshipped. But I think the reality of Isaiah 14 is that Satan is in rebellion and his ultimate objective is something much more insidious than vain worship.

Satan wants to be the chief law giver!

Those in Matthew 7 are not just preachers who were sinful and therefore rejected. I believe they had, perhaps unwittingly, joined the rebellion.

The sin of tolerance has infected the church and those who willingly tolerate this rebellion are often doing it in "the name of Jesus." This great sin of tolerance is the foundation of the satanic One World Church - which appears not as satanic but as Christian.

We are even told by the Apostle Paul,

> *"For such are false apostles, deceitful workers, transforming themselves into the apostles of Christ. And no marvel; for Satan himself is transformed into an angel of light. Therefore it is no great thing if his ministers also be transformed as the ministers of righteousness; whose end shall be according to their works."*
>
> 2 Corinthians 11:13 -15.

Compare to Matthew 7:21-23.

In spite of this warning from the Apostle Paul, many Christians foolishly look for the evil which is attacking our faith to come out of sinful places. They look at the pornographic industry, abortion mills, movie industry, drug dealers, television, evil dictators, crooked politicians, nightclubs, etc. But instead of looking at these and other obvious places of iniquity they should be looking at the church. It is in the church where the seeds of rebellion are nourished under the guise of Christianity, brotherhood and tolerance. Remember what Christ through the Apostle said: *"For such are false apostles, deceitful workers, transforming themselves into the apostles of Christ."*

There are two sins and only two which are the stepping stones into this One World Church.

And it makes no difference how many times you claim to love Jesus, or perhaps as a preacher how many times you give the altar call, sing Christian songs or pray until your throat is raw. If you embrace either one or both of these sins or have voiced tolerance to them, then you have entered the One World Church.

The two sins are homosexuality and race-mixing!

15

Whoa! I can already hear a Judeo-Christian preacher calling me an agent of Satan because I dare point out this vile iniquity!

Let me explain why I can make such a bold statement.

I know all normal, traditional Christians of the old school will agree with me, but there is a growing movement known as Racial Reconciliation which seeks to undermine the faith of our fathers. Their agenda is to replace the traditional teaching of the Christian Church with their New Age doctrine. They are working tirelessly to create a multi-racial "Christian" church. This multi-racial church IS the One World Church.

HOW CAN THAT BE?

Jesus Christ actually tells us in the Bible that the growing acceptance of these two vile sins of race-mixing and homosexuality will be the sign indicating the end of this evil age.

The cup of iniquity will be full when race mixing and homosexuality become tolerated. Before I give supporting scripture for my above statement, I want you to consider the following.

When a child is born it has ONLY two identities given to it by nature (God). The child is not born a Republican or a Democrat. The child is not born a lawyer, dentist, bus driver, carpenter, fireman, country music star or teacher. All these things which we normally use to identify someone are identifying characteristics added to the child later in life.

When you see a newborn child, you do not see a soldier, you do not see a mechanic, you do not see a policeman, you do not see a book keeper or a cosmetologist. You see either a boy or girl and you see its race. As an illustration, look at your birth certificate. It will give the baby's race and its gender. The child comes into the world with its race and its gender. Nothing else!

These two marks are determined by God. All other identifying marks are added by man.

RACE and GENDER are also the keys of understanding the last days and the One World Church!

Jesus Christ tells us there are two things we must look for in the last days, two things which evidently fill the cup of iniquity and which are now upon us. I know preachers will tell us of the signs of the last days. They will point to widespread sin and corruption. Or

16

they will tell us that the Jews are going back to the Holy Land and so this is a great sign of the last days. But the two things Jesus actually said to look for are totally ignored by virtually every preacher.

In Matthew 24, Jesus Christ tells us of the last days. Here is what He said.

> 1) "As it was in the days of Noah, so shall it be also in the days of the Son of man. "
>
> 2) "Likewise also as it was in the days of Lot ... Even thus shall it be in the day when the Son of man is revealed."

There they are, the two distinct signs to look for before the great Day of Judgment. The corruption of the world will become as it was in the days of Noah! And, as it was in the days of Lot!

I am aware there are some general things we can look at and some national events which occur. He did tell us about how and when the fig tree would put forth leaves only, it was a sign that the end is near. But here are two signs that don't just say the end in near. They tell us the end IS UPON US! Just like judgment was upon those at the time of Noah and upon those at the time of Lot.

But what did those people at Noah's time and Lot's time DO? Why was their sin any worse than the sin of mankind at any other time? Are the rejected preachers repeating the same sins that were in the day of Noah and in the day of Lot?

Here is what I suggest.

It is the "Christian" church which will bring about the One World Church. It will be through this "Christian" church that we will see the spiritual completion of Satan's rebellion.

Stay with me on this!

Rabbi Martin Seigel described the purpose of this One World Church in 1972 (New York Magazine, Jan 18).

> "I am devoting my lecture in this seminar to a discussion of the possibility that we are now entering a Jewish century, a time when the spirit of the community, the non-ideological blend of the emotional and rational and the resistance to categories and forms will emerge through the forces of anti-nationalism to provide us with a new kind of society. I call this process the Judaization of Christianity because Christianity will be the vehicle through which this society becomes Jewish."

Rabbi Martin Seigel reveals that it is this new Christianity ("new kind of society") which will bring about a Jewish world. It is this false Christian church from which the anti-Christ one world government will arise and not from the traditional sources of evil - but from the church! The Christian Church has become imbued with the teachings of Judaism. Not that it attacks Jesus Christ - by no means - it lifts up the name of Jesus Christ. But remember Satan wants to become the chief lawgiver. It is not important who you say you love but whose law you obey! Look what the Apostle Paul writes in Romans 6:16.

> *"Know ye not, that to whom ye yield yourselves servants to obey, his servants ye are to whom ye obey; whether of sin unto death" or of obedience unto righteousness?"*

The New Living Translation says it this way.

> *"Don't you realize that whatever you choose to obey becomes your master?"*

Paul makes it clear that your master is the one you are willing to obey.

Judeo-Christian ministers who support *either or both* - racial integration, reconciliation or the homosexual agenda are serving the rebellion of Satan and the One World Church. They are servants of Satan, even though they present themselves as Christian ministers and evangelists. (See II Corinthians 11:13-15) Paul said if you serve Satan you *belong* to Satan and your claims of loving Jesus, doing many wonderful works and casting out demons (making converts) will not earn you entrance to the Kingdom of God. It is for this reason that while Judeo-Christians make the show of loving Jesus they will be rejected by the One they claim to serve.

At birth every child entering the world has two identities designed by the Almighty.

Its racial identity and its sexual identity.

Race-mixing and homosexuality are a sin against nature and God's design. Jesus Christ said these two sins will become fashionable at the close of this age. The One World Government will give the legal justification for it and the One World Church through its promotion of tolerance will give the moral justification for these vile sins.

The Bible tells us of how in the final judgment there will be those standing before God enumerating all the great things and mighty works they have done in the name of Jesus.

I can imagine that these mighty works could be such things as a large church, radio stations, a Christian school or university, missionary programs, vacation Bible schools, books they have written, TV programs or satellite stations proclaiming the "gospel." If you will take time to read Matthew. 7:21-23 again, you will see that they *protested* their rejection by Christ. It is important to note this because they TRULY believed they were teaching the gospel.

They were wrong!

Keep in mind it is not because they were members of the "wrong" denomination but because they were sabotaging the mandates of nature - race and/or gender!

The Days of Noah & Lot are NOW upon US!

Earlier we examined the probability that the "anti-Christ" will be a "Christian." This modern "Christian" church marks the appearing of the One World Church. It challenges our faith and moral principle laid down in the laws of our forefathers as they desired to walk after the counsel of God.

It will be through this "Christian" church that we will see the spiritual completion of Satan's rebellion.

I want you to read *again* the words of Rabbi Martin Seigel as he describes the purpose of this One World Church (New York Magazine, Jan 18, 1972).

"I am devoting my lecture in this seminar to a discussion of the possibility that we are now entering a Jewish century, a time when the spirit of the community, the non-ideological blend of the emotional and rational and the resistance to categories and forms will emerge through the forces of anti-nationalism to provide us with a new kind of society. I call this process the Judaization of Christianity because Christianity will be the vehicle through which this society becomes Jewish."

It is this false Christian church from which the anti-Christ one world government will arise and not from the traditional sources of evil - but from the church! The "Christian Church" has become "Jewish" - that is anti-Christ. Not that it attacks Jesus Christ - by no means - it lifts up the name of Jesus Christ. But remember Satan wants to become the chief lawgiver. It is not important who you say you love but whose law you obey! The words of Apostle Paul are clear.

"Know ye not, that to whom ye yield yourselves servants to obey, his servants ye are to whom ye obey; whether of sin unto death" or of obedience unto righteousness?"

Romans 6:16

The New Living Translation says,

20

"Don't you realize that whatever you choose to obey becomes your master?"

AS IT WAS IN THE DAYS OF LOT

Jesus said at the close of this final age we would have a repeat of what happened in the days of Noah and what happened in the days of Lot.

> *"And as it was in the days of Noe, so shall it be also in the days of the Son of man. They did eat, they drank, they married wives, they were given in marriage, until the day that Noe entered into the ark, and the flood came, and destroyed them all. Likewise also as it was in the days of Lot; they did eat, they builded."*
>
> Luke 17:26-28

I am aware that most preachers will gloss over this important statement of Jesus and simply say, *"It's going to become a really wicked time,"* as it was in Noah's day and as it was in Lot's day.

Sure it will become wicked but what specifically were they **DOING** at the time of Noah and at the time of Lot? The answer is simple. At the time of Noah they were practicing race-mixing and at the time of Lot they were practicing homosexuality, both in violation of the mandates of nature - race and gender!

Let's look at the days of Lot first because most everyone is well aware that homosexuality was the sin of Sodom and Gomorrah. In fact, it was from this sinful city of Sodom where we get the word sodomy to describe homosexuality. They were homosexuals. Let's read a portion of the account from Genesis 19:4-5.

> *"But before they lay down, the men of the city, even the men of Sodom, compassed the house round, both old and young, all the people from every quarter: And they called unto Lot, and said unto him, Where are the men which came in to thee this night? bring them out unto us, that we may know them."*

Let's look at how two other translations render this passage.

> *"Before they had gone to bed, all the young and old male citizens of Sodom surrounded the house. They called to Lot, 'Where are the men who came to [stay with] you tonight? Bring them out to us so that we can have sex with them."*
>
> God's Word Translation

It is clear from this passage in the three translations presented that homosexuality was the sin of Sodom. Jesus said this great sin of Sodomy (homosexuality) would become a sign of the last days.

AS IT WAS IN THE DAYS OF NOAH

The other sign that we would see is the sin of race-mixing or miscegenation - as it was in the days of Noah!

I know that a growing number of churches bow to the New Age god of Racial Reconciliation and it is because they are part of the One World Church. I know they will deny it, but it is still the truth. They give prophesy (teach) in the name of Jesus, they cast out devils (make converts) in the name of Jesus and they do many wonderful works in the name of Jesus. In fact, looking at their cosmetics (their outward appearance) they are wonderful, spirit filled, born-again Christians, but the fact is they have become tolerant of Satan's rebellion against God and his natural law and therefore, will meet Jesus Christ in the "board room" and hear the words,

"You're fired! . . . Depart from me for I never knew you!"

Our lives are to be guided by *principle*, not *emotion*. I have heard stories of people who said they fell in "love" with a non-white and the excuse is given, "He (or she) is a wonderful Christian." But does being a "wonderful" Christian change Godly principle?

Here is an illustration. We all know cheating on your spouse is not only "wrong" in the eyes of the world, it is sin in the eyes of God. But what if the person you want to *cheat* with is a "wonderful" Christian, would it then be OK? Of course not! It would be a violation of Godly principle. The same is true with interracial dating and marriage. The claim that the non-White boy or girl is a "wonderful" Christian does not change Godly principle - no matter how nice, kind and wonderful the person may be.

Remember Jesus said, *"As it was in the days of Lot"* and *"as it was in the days of Noah."* I think it is quite clear that when Jesus said *"as it was in the days of Lot"* He is making reference to the accep-

22

tance and toleration of homosexuality. So, likewise, when Jesus said *"as it was in the days of Noah,"* He is making reference to the acceptance and toleration of interracial marriage.

Let me tell you what the Bible says even though Judeo-Christian preachers, out of ignorance or deceit, will not tell you.

At the time of Noah all of society had engaged in wholesale race-mixing, promoted race-mixing or were tolerant of race-mixing. The children of Adam had married into the pre-Adamic races of people.

Ok! I know all you Judeo-Christians are getting bent out of shape and will start telling me that the Bible says that Adam was the first man on the earth.

Actually the Bible doesn't say that!

If you think it does - send me a letter and tell me where!

If you are a closed minded New Age Judeo-Christian I probably already lost you anyway. But if you are open-minded and willing to be lead by the Holy Spirit - read on!

The sin of race-mixing was the dominate sin that brought about the flood and is easily shown from scripture.

> *"And it came to pass, when men began to multiply on the face of the earth, and daughters were born unto them, That the sons of God saw the daughters of men that they were fair; and they took them wives of all which they chose. And the LORD said, My spirit shall not always strive with man, for that he also is flesh: yet his days shall be an hundred and twenty years.*
>
> *"There were giants in the earth in those days; and also after that, when the sons of God came in unto the daughters of men, and they bare children to them, the same became mighty men which were of old, men of renown. And GOD saw that the wickedness of man was great in the earth, And that every imagination of the thoughts of his heart was only evil continually. And it repented the LORD that he had made man on the earth, and it grieved him at his heart. And the LORD said, I will destroy man whom I have created from the face of the earth; both man, and beast, and the creeping thing, and the fowls of the air; for it repenteth me that I have made them.*
>
> *"But Noah found grace in the eyes of the LORD. These are the generations of Noah: Noah was a just man and perfect in his generations, and Noah walked with God."*
>
> Genesis 6: 1-9

Bible scholars have debated as to who the sons of God and the daughters of men were. Some have claimed the daughters of men are the daughters of Adam and the sons of God are fallen angels. Other have speculated that the sons of God were the children of Adam and the daughters of men are of the pre-Adamic creation. Scholars can debate this until the cows come home, however, the fact is, regardless of who was who, the message is clear - unlawful marriages took place.

Then we read,

> "But Noah found grace in the eyes of the LORD. These are the gener-
> ations of Noah: Noah was a just man and perfect in his generations,
> and Noah walked with God."

We won't dispute the fact that Noah was a righteous man, but there is something else happening here that is often overlooked. Noah was a "just man," yes, Noah, "walked with God," yes. But he was also *"perfect in his generations."* If we want to understand what was happening here we need to look at two keys words - perfect and generations.

The Hebrew word for perfect is *tamiym*. But don't rely upon my interpretation of this word, rather look at the definition that the trusted scholar James Strong gives in his Strong's Concordance of the Bible.

> PERFECT - tamiym, "entire (literally, figuratively or morally); also (as
> noun) integrity, truth,: - without blemish, complete, full, perfect, sincere-
> ly (-ity), sound, without spot, undefiled, upright (-ly), whole."

Judeo-Christians will tell us that Noah was saved from the flood because he was a good, righteous, moral man. And indeed he was, because the Bible tells us he *"walked with God."* However, it also says he was undefiled, without spot and without blemish. While the word can be used to describe a moral condition (which is the only meaning Judeo-Christians want to give), it also is used to describe a literal condition.

Is it possible that with all flesh having corrupted itself (see vs. 12) that Noah and his family were the last of the Adamic people who were racially undefiled? Or perhaps there were others who were racially undefiled, but whose spirit was corrupted. They were committed to the teachings of tolerance and were part of the rebellion and therefore, did not "walk with God."

__Keep in mind that there are only two identifying factors given to a newborn child: its race and its gender.__

Both of which were created by God. Proper understanding of race and gender are the foundation of the nuclear family and thus civilization.

Sodomy and Miscegenation are abominations which destroy the mandates of nature and they have entered the Church and now stand in the Holy place. New Age Judeo-Christian churches which ignore one or both of these God-given mandates are fellow travelers of Satan's rebellion and are a part of the One World Church of Babylon even though they may be totally unaware of their involvement.

Jesus said in the end of time we would see a return to the days of Noah and the days of Lot.

With Lot it was sexual perversion and with Noah it was racial perversion. Satan is in rebellion to God and churches which teach either acceptance of homosexuality or racial reconciliation or both have joined the rebellion.

Noah was undefiled, without blemish in his generation. The English word generation used here in verse 9 comes from the Hebrew word *towldah*

> *"Noah was a just man and perfect in his generations* (towldah)*, and Noah walked with God."*

Lets go back again and see how Hebrew scholar, James Strong defines the word *towldah*.

"descent, ie. family: history, birth - generations."

The root word is yalad - *"to bear young, to show lineage, bring forth children"*

It is also interesting to note that the Hebrew word towlad shares the same root word (yalad) as towldah. Towlad means posterity. Yalad the root word for both towlad and towldah, according to James Strong in his Concordance of the Bible, means to bear young, to beget, show lineage, to bring forth children.

There is no question that the word generation means - family descent, family lineage, posterity, etc. In other words, Noah was without blemish in his ancestry. His family lineage was undefiled. Some may not like it - but the fact is Noah and his family were delivered from the flood because physically they were not racially mixed and spiritually they were intolerant of miscegenation.

> *The days of Lot were the practice of and tolerance of Sodomy.*
> *The days of Noah were the practice of and tolerance of race-mixing.*

The days of Noah and the days of Lot are upon us. The great multitude of Judeo-Christian churches has bowed before the great god of tolerance.

As homosexual, lesbian and transgender misfits gain acceptance by the national media, television, magazines and Hollywood, they will eventually gain civil rights protection from the federal government. When that happens, Judeo-Christian churches will bow before the "law" and welcome them into their church. To safeguard their tax exempt status they will first become silent, then they will become self-righteous in their silence, then they will become tolerant, then they will grant acceptance. At that point they will claim those who do not accept homosexuals into their families, churches and communities are narrow-minded *unchristian* bigots.

How do I know? Because they went through the same process toward the acceptance of miscegenation. And now the gay agenda is following the same path and the church will not be able to stand strong. They have already *proven* they are weak and cannot muster the spiritual strength to remain strong to the faith of their forefathers.

HOW HAS THE JUDEO-CHRISTIAN CHURCH DEMONSTRATED ITS WEAKNESS?

The church stood against racial integration and intermarriage until they were threatened with the loss of their tax exemption. Today, the very same churches who spoke against interracial marriage are now tolerant of it and will not speak against it. Because we know Judeo-Christians have proven their weakness on the issues of race, (we have no guide by which to judge the future but from the past) we can say with a certain degree of confidence that they will

26

also bow before homosexual demands and eventually grant tolerance and acceptance.

Don't tell me it won't happen or your church is different - Jesus Christ said it would. The days of Noah and The days of Lot are upon us.

If you attend or financially support a Judeo-Christian church you need to remove yourself from it as soon as possible or else you may be pulled into their delusion. As Christians, we must be careful to guard our lives from the deception of the Judeo-Christian rebellion against God.

The CHRISTIAN CHURCH Is now Jewish

Although I am unaware of any Scripture which would either support or refute my next statement, I am of the opinion that this One World Church is not necessarily ONE organization. Contrary to the teaching of most prophetic preachers, the One World Church does not have one central authority.

In other words, different church denominations can be members of the One World Church while maintaining their separate identities or denominational headquarters.

They have become a part of the One World Church because they have abandoned the natural law (race and gender) of the Creator and teach or tolerate the sins which dominated and brought about the judgment of God in the days of Noah and in the days of Lot.

The One World Church professes Christianity but promotes tolerance toward "miscegenation" and a tolerance toward sodomy. It has become indoctrinated and intoxicated with the teachings of the rabbis. Jesus warned His disciples in Scripture to beware of the leaven (teaching) of the Pharisees in Matthew 16:6-12. (When I do it I am called an anti-Semitic bigot!)

"Then Jesus said unto them, Take heed and beware of the leaven of the Pharisees and of the Sadducees. And they reasoned among themselves, saying, It is because we have taken no bread. Which when Jesus perceived, he said unto them, O ye of little faith, why reason ye among yourselves, because ye have brought no bread? Do ye not understand, neither remember the five loaves of the five thousand, and how many baskets ye took up? Neither the seven loaves of the four thousand, and how many baskets ye took up? How is it that ye do not understand that I spake it not to you concerning bread, neither ye should beware of the leaven of the Pharisees and the Sadducees? Then understood they how that he bade them not beware of the leaven of bread, but of the doctrine of the Pharisees and of the Sadducees."

Jesus was telling His disciples that the doctrine (religion) of the Pharisees was deadly. Just as leaven (yeast) would expand into a loaf of bread, so would the doctrine of the Pharisees expand and destroy them. They must be careful because if they were not, this insidious Pharisee religion would grow among them and corrupt the Gospel.

THE CHRISTIAN CHURCH CORRUPTED

This is exactly what is happening today: the doctrines of the Pharisees have corrupted the Christian faith, preparing it for the One World Church. In Titus 1:14, the Apostle Paul also warned us about "Jewish fables" infiltrating the church. This infiltration of Jewish doctrine and fables into the Christian church is what corrupted and destroyed it. From out of its dead body a new church, embracing the Jewish doctrine of tolerance, has arisen.

This is why the Jewish Rabbi Martin Seigel could boast,

> *"Christianity will be the vehicle through which this society becomes Jewish."*

The rebellion of Satan is going to enhance its power, not through the "dens of iniquity" but through the CHRISTIAN CHURCH! Of course, the church will not be truly Christian, even though it will still teach in the name of Jesus, cast out devils, win converts and perform many wonderful works in the name of Jesus, (see Matthew. 7:21-23). All this is necessary to empower the great deception of the new One World Church of tolerance. This One World Church now has total toleration and acceptance of interracial marriage and has almost total toleration (though not yet total acceptance) of homosexuality. I have often been criticized by Judeo-Christians for exposing the treachery of Judaism.

However, the fact is that we have Jesus Christ as our example and *His* intolerance to Pharisaism.

In fact, the hatred of the Pharisee Jews against Jesus was so intense that Jesus Christ eventually avoided ministering in Judea because the Jews wanted to kill him, John 7:1.

A reading of Matthew 23 will quickly reveal the harsh and unkind words Jesus spoke toward the Pharisees. I will give one example in verses 27-28,

> "Woe unto you scribes and Pharisees, hypocrites! for ye are like unto whited sepulchres, which indeed appear beautiful outward, but are within full of dead men's bones, and of all uncleanness. Even so ye also outwardly appear righteous unto men, but within ye are full of hypocrisy and iniquity. "

Ministers and church leaders are certainly aware of these "hateful" words of Jesus but will gloss over them claiming that He was addressing His remarks only to those Pharisees who stood before him.

But that is a foolish thing to say. Jesus made it clear - it was the ***doctrine*** of the Pharisees - and this doctrine of the Pharisees is ***still*** the teaching of modern Judaism.

The dominant religion of Jesus' day was Pharisaism. This Pharisee religion had its origin in Babylon and the holy book used by these Pharisees was the Babylonian Talmud. Babylon is the name given to this satanic rebellion, (Isaiah 14) which is the birth mother of all filthiness and whoredoms. Read Revelation 17 & 18.

The same Jewish (Pharisee) religion which brought about the crucifixion of Jesus Christ (thinking they could kill God) is the same Jewish religion which today profits from war, pornography, terror, moral corruption, international finance and all manner of filthiness. Those who disagree with me are again at odds with Scripture. I want to point out once again that this Jewish religion based upon the Babylonian Talmud, according to Scripture, is the cesspool from which all manner of filth and corruption comes. (Note Revelation 17& 18).

All students of the Scriptures are aware that the Bible identifies Babylon as the adversary of Jesus Christ and His saints. Babylon is the name all Christians associate with the anti-Christ. But what many do not know is that this Jewish (Pharisee) religion did not have its origin among the ancient Hebrews but its origin was in Babylon!

Many Christians believe that the only difference between Christianity and the Jewish religion is: we believe both the Old and New Testaments are divinely inspired, whereas it is their understanding that the Jewish religion is based on the teachings of the Old Testament only. But that is not a correct understanding. The Pharisee (Jewish) religion actually has the Talmud as the foundation of their religious doctrine. And the rabbis use the Talmud (which they hold in higher authority) to interpret the Old Testament. But if we want to be accurate, the full and complete name of the "Holy" book of the Pharisee (Jewish) religion is not The Talmud!

On the next page I have reprinted the front page of the "Talmud" and you will note its correct and accurate name is -The Babylonian Talmud!

The origin of the Talmud was in Babylon with new text being added to it by rabbis up through the 8th century AD. During the time of Christ it was called, *The Traditions of the Elders*. Here is what noted rabbinical scholar Rabbi Michael L. Rodkinson says about the Talmud.

"The Talmud is, then, the written form of that which in the time of Jesus, was called the Traditions of the Elders."

It is this Babylonian Talmud which provides the inspiration for Mystery Babylon - and the One World Church. This Babylonian Pharisee (Jewish) religion is clearly recognized by Jesus Christ as vile, rotten and corrupt. See Matthew 23.

The Jewish Talmud came out of Babylon!

Throughout Scripture we are able to see the extreme hatred the Pharisees had for Jesus Christ.

This hatred was so passionate that they were able to eventually frame him on false charges which brought about His execution on Calvary. This same hatred has continued to this very day. Remember, the hatred of Jesus Christ (and His followers) is at the center of the Satanic rebellion. An example of this hate is revealed in the writings of the late prize winning Hollywood script writer and book author Ben Hecht. In 1931 he authored and published, *A Jew in Love*. I have a copy of this rare book in my library. In his book, his hatred for Jesus Christ is clearly shown as he fantasizes about the crucifixion with a vile description of how he would have handled it.

NEW EDITION

OF THE

BABYLONIAN TALMUD

Original Text Edited, Corrected, Formulated, and
Translated into English

BY

MICHAEL L. RODKINSON

First Edition Revised and Corrected

BY

THE REV. DR. ISAAC M. WISE
President Hebrew Union College, Cincinnati, O.

Volume I.
TRACT SABBATH

SECOND EDITION, RE-EDITED, REVISED AND ENLARGED

BOSTON

> *"One of the finest things ever done by the mob was the the crucifixion of Jesus Christ. Intellectually it was a splendid gesture. But trust the mob to bungle. If I have had charge of the executing Christ, I'd have handled it differently. You see, what I would have done was had him shipped to Rome and fed to the lions. They could never have made a savior out of mince meat. I would do the same thing to the radicals today."*
>
> A Jew In Love - Page 21

This hatred directed against Jesus Christ by the mob which screamed, howled and screeched, *"Crucify Him, crucify Him!"* continues to this very day. It's the same bunch!

Foolish Judeo-Christians think that this Pharisee religion was simply an extreme, self-righteous form of the temple worship of the Israelites. However, this is not true. It was an entirely *different* religion of Babylonian origin and was not the religion of the patriarchs. Babylonian Pharisaism had swallowed up the Scriptural teachings of the true Israelites in much the same way it is now swallowing up the Christian faith of today, altering it into Judeo-Christianity

> Judeo-Christians who defend Judaism are defending the very ones Jesus condemned.

which reaches out to embrace both miscegenation and sodomy.

All this is important if we are going to understand the nature of the One World Church.

Judaism, as it exists today, is the same Pharisee religion that was in existence at the time of Jesus Christ.

Pharisaism and Judaism are the SAME. Both are corrupt. Both are vile. Both represent the rebellion of Satan and both are under the condemnation of Jesus Christ.

Judeo-Christians who defend Judaism are defending the very ones Jesus condemned.

The fact that Pharisaism and Judaism is the same thing is self-evident. However, for those who are doubters I want to offer the following evidence.

The 1943 edition of the Universal Jewish Encyclopedia says under the heading of Pharisees the following.

"The Jewish religion as it is today traces its descent, without a break, through all the centuries from the Pharisees."

I have in my library the 1965 edition of *The Encyclopedia of the Jewish Religion*. This encyclopedia was compiled by 21 rabbis and scholars of the Jewish religion and its production was aided by The Jewish Theological Seminary of New York. I want you to know that this is a work of immense authority. In other words, it's the real deal. Those that doubt what we are saying can't claim that it's an obscure writing.

This is what it says under Pharisee.

"The Pharisaic line was continued by Talmudic and later rabbis, who together form the tradition of rabbinic Judaism, so that the entire subsequent development of Judaism bears the indelible stamp of Pharisaism."

Rabbi Louis Finklestein of the Jewish Theological Seminary (New York) wrote in his book *The Pharisees*:

"Pharisaism became Talmudism, Talmudism became Medieval Rabbinism, and Medieval Rabbinism became Modern Rabbinism. But throughout these changes of name . . . the spirit of the ancient Pharisees survives unaltered."

Could anything be more clearly stated? Jewish scholars freely and willingly admit that Judaism is Pharisaism. Yet Christians who speak against Jewish (Pharisee) corruption in the same manner as Jesus did are called hateful bigots by Judeo-Christians who have been spiritually weakened by the leaven of the Pharisees.

The modern church and its leaders regularly and boastfully profess they are grounded on Judeo-Christian principles. But these formerly Christian churches are part of the rebellion and part of the One World Church.

The **Last** Church

"miserable, wretched, poor, blind and naked"

Many Bible scholars consider the seven churches of Revelation 2 and 3 to be a history of the church from the time of Christ to the present. If this is true then the last church before the final judgment is the Laodicean church. This would then be the church that is now upon us and would be the final church before its absorption into the One World Church.

The first thing we want to understand is that this Laodicean church is the church of tolerance.

TOLERANCE IS THE GATEWAY

to the One World Church. As we have stated previously, contrary to the teaching of Judeo-Christianity, tolerance is *not* a Christian character. However, Judeo-Christian churches continually pound into the hearts of their followers that they should be men and women of tolerance - *just like Jesus Christ*. In fact, not only are they told to be tolerant, they are also told intolerance is sinful and of the devil. I have discussed this earlier and have attempted to show that it is true that as a Christian you are to have tolerance toward other Christians who may have a different doctrinal viewpoint than you have. However, we are not to be tolerant toward heathen anti-Christian religions. We are not to back away from our Christian faith in our schools or in our city, state or national governments.

Tolerance is a tool used against Christians to weaken their resolve. By this means Christians remove the walls and barriers which keep out sin. Because of our desire to be tolerant "like Jesus" we have welcomed heathen gods and their non-Christian standards into our nation, our government, our schools, our churches and into our homes. Tolerance is the poison which is spewed from the

35

teachings of the rabbis. Not that they practice tolerance themselves. On the contrary. The Jewish Pharisee religion is very intolerant to the true, Biblical faith. The sin of tolerance is one of the fables and Pharisee doctrines which we were warned about by Jesus and the Apostle Paul. According to the teachings of the Pharisees, it is OK for us to believe Jesus was a good man, but don't belittle other religions, or put forth the silly notion that Jesus Christ is the ONE and ONLY true God. To do that would be insensitive to other religions - it would be un-kind, hateful, intolerant and unchristian. The fact is, Jesus Christ was very intolerant and said there was only ONE road to heaven and it was a narrow (intolerant?) road, but the road to destruction is a wide road and there are many who travel this road.

> The sin of tolerance is one of the fables and doctrines we were warned about Jesus Christ and the Apostle Paul.

> *"Enter ye in at the strait gate: for wide is the gate, and broad is the way, that leadeth to destruction, and many there be which go in thereat: Because strait is the gate, and narrow is the way, which leadeth unto life, and few there be that find it,"*
>
> Matthew. 7:13.

Judeo-Christian churches are parroting the teachings of the rabbis and while claiming they want to teach Jesus, are very careful not to offend those who practice heathen religions. They ought to think a little more of whether or not they are offending the holiness of God by their teachings of tolerance.

THE LAODICEAN CHURCH

It is important for us to look at this Laodicean Church of Revelation 3:14-21. The Laodicean Church is the last church before the final judgment from God. It is a church of immense tolerance. We are told that though it is powerful and rich it is *"miserable, wretched, poor, blind and naked,"* vs. 17. What an accurate description of the modern super churches growing in America today. One example of the super church is the Lakeside Church in Houston, Texas, pastored by Joel Osteen. This church has grown to a membership of 30,000 and boasts that it is one of America's most "diverse churches." And this is just one of many super churches throughout the country.

Every one of these super churches supports racial integration and most are soft on homosexuality. It isn't their size or wealth that qualifies them as a member of the One World Church, but rather their permissive doctrine of tolerance.

Does that mean everything these churches teach is bad? Of course not! Many people have fooled themselves into thinking that these churches are crusaders of the Gospel. But the problem is people are looking at them through the eyes of sinful flesh. For where they see much good - God sees much evil. So much so that when the ministers of the Judeo-Christian churches stand before Him in judgment he will say, *"Depart from me for I never knew you!"* Matthews 7:22-23. Why? Because they will not speak out against the sin of race-mixing and few even dare to speak of the evils of sodomy. When we look at verses 15 and 16 of Revelation 3, we quickly discover that the great sins of this repugnant church is that it is tolerant and it has no backbone!

> *"And unto the angel of the church of the Laodiceans write . . . I know thy works, that thou art neither cold nor hot: I would thou wert cold or hot. So then because thou art lukewarm and neither cold nor hot I will spue thee out of my mouth."*

This church is lukewarm. The Greek word for lukewarm is *chliaros* and means to be tepid. This Laodicean (Judeo-Christian) church has no real emotional hatred for the evil and corruption which is befalling our nation. It takes a ho hum attitude. They want to be liked and admired by the world. But God's people who really and truly love God must equally have real gut wrenching hatred for evil.

It is not enough to be against evil, God expects you to *hate* wickedness with passion - with intensity!

The vile sins of race-mixing and homosexuality, the sins of Noah's day and of Lot's day are upon us. But Judeo-Christian churches are more concerned with putting on the robes of love, brotherhood and tolerance than the robes of righteousness.

VOMIT NOT SPIT

God tells these Judeo-Christians, who take pride in their tolerance, *"I am going to spue you out of my mouth."* Most people, when reading this, think it means God is going to *spit* these lukewarm people out of his mouth. But that is not exactly what it says. The word spue is from the Greek word *emeo* and it doesn't mean spit, it means vomit. Certainly you know the difference. It is our nature to spit something out of our mouth the moment we know it is spoiled or tastes bad. It is an immediate reaction. But to vomit, that only comes after our stomach has become sick. And usually we try to avoid it as long as possible, but then suddenly we can't hold it any longer and we vomit - uncontrollably.

This is exactly what is being said here. God is looking at this Laodicean (Judeo-Christian) church and He has endured much patience with its wickedness - its tolerance - its tolerance for sin and its tolerance for the rebellion! But, just like when you are sick to your stomach - God is trying to keep from throwing up. Use your imagination for a moment and clearly picture someone in your mind who is in the midst of vomiting. Visualize this in slow motion. Their face is contorted, the mouth is gaped open and the contents of their stomach is heaving forth. It's a pretty disgusting sight. Well, the Judeo-Christian church is literally making God sick to His stomach and He will eventually spue (vomit) out the filth He can no longer contain.

This Laodicean church receives its name from Laodicea, a city in Asia Minor. The city was founded about 261 BC by Antiochus II who named the city Laodicea, in honor of his wife.

Bible students will note that Laodicea was a wealthy city, on major trade routes and the location of many banking institutions. In 60 AD the city was struck by a major earthquake, but because of its immense wealth it refused a government earthquake relief offer.

All this is interesting, but it's the *NAME* (which has been overlooked by Bible scholars) which carries so much vital importance to our study of the One World Church.

WHAT IS THE LAODICEAN CHURCH?

God knows what He is doing and this last vile church with its putrid doctrine of tolerance for race-mixing and its soft condemnation of homosexuality is appropriately named.

Like all names, this church name, Laodicea, has a meaning. The Greek word for Laodicea is *Laodikeia*. Dr. James Strong tells us in his Strong's Concordance of the Bible that Laodicea was a city in Asia Minor. But he also tells us that the word is a combination of two other words.

The two words when combined form the word *Laodicea* are Laos and *dike*. The meaning of the word *laos* is set forth by Dr. Strong to be,

> *"a people (in general, thus* differing *from "demos. "which denotes one's own populace) - a people."*

Understand what Dr. Strong is saying here. Demos means *"one's OWN people."*

The word *laos* in laodicean means *other people* who are *not* of "one 's own people." In other words it means people other than your own people! The second half of the word is *dike* and it means *"right (as self-evident) i.e. justice (the principle, a decision, or its execution)."*

God is telling us that this last church, this vile, weak, Judeo-Christian, Laodicean church has become the church of *other people's* rights which disregard the New Covenant God made with Israel through the sacrifice of His body and blood. This Laodicean

> *Tolerance is a tool used against Christians to weaken their resolve*

Church is literally a **multi-racial** church (a church for everybody) which is now quickly becoming tolerant of homosexuality and will in time grant full acceptance. Through the One World, Judeo-Christian, Laodicean Church, Satan not only continues to challenge God's natural law governing race and gender, but any law or symbolism which trumpets the authority of God. The Church of Jesus Christ, except for a remnant which has remained faithful, has been changed by the doctrine (leaven) of the Pharisees into this Laodicean Church. This Laodicean Church is the New Age, multi-racial One World Church. *It's the last church* and it's on your TV, in your community and at your doorstep.

The preachers spoken of in Matthew 7:21-23 are preachers who pretend and perhaps actually believe they are ministers of God. They protested God's condemnation of them and their ministry pointing out the many wonderful things they have done in the name of Jesus Christ. But we are reminded of this very same bunch in II Timothy 3. Here we are told that they have a form of Godliness but deny His power and authority - as they merrily go their way down the wide road of destruction.

> *"This know also, that in the last days perilous times shall come. For men shall be lovers of their own selves, boasters, proud, blasphemers, disobedient to parents, unthankful, unholy, Without natural affection, . . . Traitors, heady, high-minded, lovers of pleasures more than lovers of God; Having a form of godliness, but denying the power thereof: from such turn away."*

Warning!
To parents •

I would strongly advise parents not to allow their children to attend Sunday School, church or the Vacation Bible Schools of churches which promote the Racial Reconciliation cult.

Of course they will make the attempt to shame you into thinking the reason you do not want them attending is because you are afraid of their teachings. The fact is, you *are* afraid of their teaching. As parents, not only do you have the awesome responsibility to protect your children from physical danger but from moral and spiritual danger as well. You accomplish this by giving them solid Biblical Christian training. We are told in scripture (Proverbs 22:6),

> "Train up a child in the way he should go: and when he is old, he will not depart from it."

I would not allow my children to go the religious meetings of Spiritualists, Hindoos or Buddhists, so why would I allow them to attend church services of racial reconciliators just because they have a veneer of Christianity? I would not allow them (especially when they are very little) to go to the movies or watch TV without supervision.

The racial reconciliation cult is targeting young people through cartoons, TV, magazines, movies and religion. Parents must monitor the tv and movies their children watch and understand that the propaganda of racial reconciliation cult members is as dangerous to the spiritual welfare and Christian integrity of your child as pornography and the teachings of other occult, new age and "eastern" religions such as Spiritualists, Hindoos, Buddhists, and Islam.

Are Your Children Being Prepared for the

ONE WORLD CHURCH

I know you don't think so. After all, the ONE WORLD CHURCH is anti-Christian and you are a Christian. And you are raising your children to be Christians.

You teach them not to steal.

You teach them not to lie.

You teach them not to use drugs.

You teach them to help people.

You teach them to go to church.

You teach them to give their heart to Jesus.

You try to be a good example to them.

But what if all the above is not enough?

Actually, the above is what most people tell their kids. Oh, I know there are bad parents out there. The judicial system sees them all the time. But the fact is most parents teach their kids to be good.

But That is Not Enough!

Certainly you are aware that being "good" is a relative term. "Good" in the eyes of man and "good" in the eyes of God are not the same. And then there is the acronym WWJD that church people will wear on tee-shirts, caps, jewelry, etc. The acronym is a reminder to people that in every decision they make they will always do what Jesus would do when facing the same decision.

I don't want to make fun of the concept, because we *should* do what Jesus would do! We SHOULD guide our lives with a WWJD mentality.

But the fact is most people have no earthly idea what Jesus would do, because they make their decisions based upon their own carnal knowledge of right and wrong!

Christians usually think that because they "love" Jesus they are immune from the deception of the world. It's all those *other people,* the non-Christians, which are going to be deceived and go to hell because they got the "mark" - and joined the One World Church!

It is at this point where they will thump their Bible and say, *"It's all right here in Revelations!"*

I realize that most of you are quite aware of the enormous problem we face. The Apostle Paul pointed out that we are not fighting flesh but spiritual wickedness in high places.

> *"For we wrestle not against flesh and blood, but against principalities, against powers, against the rulers of the darkness of this world, against spiritual wickedness in high places."*
> Ephesians 6:12

It isn't you I am concerned about. I know you have already rejected the occult teachings of the modern church. However, the post "Christian" church with its Judaic teachings of tolerance has opened the doors for wide spread acceptance of miscegenation and Sodomy.

I am aware that the majority of Judeo-Christians still do not accept homosexuality (sodomy), however, the door has been opened and a new generation of kids are coming up in our "Christian" churches, which have been programmed to think that tolerance of miscegenation and homosexuality is a Christian virtue. Furthermore, they are convinced that those who do not accept a multi-racial and "gay-friendly" community and church are intolerant hateful bigots who do not possess the spirit of Christ.

While you may be safe, in that you are solid in your Christian

43

commitment to moral principle, your children are being targeted and many parents are completely unaware of how their children are being stolen out from beneath them.

Recently, I received a phone call from a young father who was totally flabbergasted when his young 7 year old daughter came home from school all excited about what a wonderful man Martin Luther King was and how we are a great country today because of men like King. He had no idea that such rubbish was being taught to his little girl. Can you imagine his horror?

Another couple, who are solid in the racialist cause and are committed to give proper teaching to their children, thought nothing of sending their children to the Bible school at a local church. After attending one Bible school session, their 5 year old son came home with a picture of Jesus which he had colored with his crayons. What shocked them was that Jesus was colored brown. Why? because that is what the teacher told them to color Jesus.

And don't forget that little girl I mentioned earlier, who was told by her Sunday school teacher that if she did not play with the new little black boy who came to church, she was making Jesus unhappy and she may not get to go to heaven. How many children are hearing this same theme day after day in school or at their church, many of whom perhaps never say anything to mom or dad? And even if they do, how many moms and dads are properly prepared to answer them. You must be aware that it is much easier to satisfy the curiosity of a 7 year old than a 16 year old. For example, mom or dad can say to the 7 year old. *"No darling, King was a bad man and the school is not telling you the truth."* The seven year old will immediately believe you and that is the end of the learning session.

However, if the child keeps hearing this year after year, at 16 they are going to want a better answer. Of course this anti-White propaganda is then enhanced by television, movies, magazines and churches. Our children are growing into young adults without any racial identity. The only identity they acquire is from MTV, black sports "heroes" and pop singers like Britney Spears.

It's no wonder we are losing this generation!

Sadly, most parents fail to understand the intensity of how their children are being targeted. All too often parents think that a few off-the-cuff remarks about minorities or homosexuals are enough to shelter their kids from the harmful effects of this new age cult which is being subtly pounded into their heads hour after hour and day after day.

Let me give you a couple of examples sent to me, via email, from young people who are boasting of their love and tolerance for all people including homosexuals.

> *"How can you actually believe that anything you say is even remotely true? I have read your website and think you are deceived by Satan. I am only 15 and even I can see how ridiculous you are. Jesus loves all people and it doesn't matter what their race is or what their sexual orientation is. Unlike you I am a REAL Christian!"*

Here is another example.

> *"I hope and pray that who ever reads this email will be convicted by the Holy Spirit to repent of your evil ways and stop hating people who are different than you. God loves ALL people! As a born-again Christian I have to rebuke you in the name of Jesus. African-Americans, Jews, Asians are loved by God as much if not more than you evil racists. And even though I don't approve of the Gay lifestyle, I still love them and have many Gay friends and they are more Christian than you."*

Why have the preachers failed to give proper teaching to these kids? It is simple: they are weak and have no backbone. The Bible says they are like dogs.

> *"His watchmen are blind, they are all ignorant, they are all dumb dogs, they cannot bark: sleeping, lying down, loving to slumber. Yea, they are greedy dogs, which can never have enough, and they are shepherds that cannot understand: they all look to their own way, every one for his gain."*

There are a multitude of preachers who fit this description. Many of them are well known and appear on television. I can name a few: Joel Osteen, John Hagee, Jimmy Swaggart, Charles Stanley Kenneth Copeland, and Benny Hinn. I could call them the *Dumb Dog Preachers* but I would be condemned for doing so. And so I won't.

Maybe I already did! Hmm!

There is a host of people who are fans of each of those I named who may get upset, but that is exactly what the Bible calls them.

When was the last time ANY of these preachers spoke out against the sins of race-mixing and sodomy?

But what about the preacher at your church? A few years ago a survey was taken asking people what they thought of our U. S. Congressmen and Senators. The answer probably will not surprise you. Most people thought politicians in general were crooks. What was amazing is that even though they thought our congressmen and senators were crooks, they also believe THEIR congressman and senator was a good and honest man.

They refused to include the congressman and senator which they voted for among the "bad guys." It was everybody else's congress-man and senator that was crooked.

I suspect the same thing applies to preachers.

What about your preacher?

I am not claiming they are thieves, at least not in the sense of stealing money out of the offering plate. But why aren't they teach-ing our kids? Why are they not speaking in defense of our national borders? Why do they not give warning to our people?

So you try to teach your kids. You make the occasional off-the-cuff remark about minorities and you think your kids will magically turn into a courageous man or woman who will not bow down to the god of racial and homosexual tolerance. All the while your children are daily programmed hour after hour by *professionals* who know exactly how to reach your kids.

I knew this one couple who had a young 16 year old girl and never brought her to any meetings and, in fact, had no idea her parents were involved in the White Nationalist cause. I always encouraged them to bring her and get her involved. But their answer was always the same. At 16, they said, she should be thinking about having fun and enjoy being a teenager and not be weighted down with the issues of the world. When she is older, they will tell her and she can make her own decision.

Well the decision will be made, but it won't be her decision. It will be the decision of those who targeted her while her parents failed their responsibility to properly raise their child.

When I was raising my children I took them to EVERYTHING. My wife and I wanted to be the ones to shape their lives and not some New Age Guru who would target them for the One World Church.

In fact, we didn't send them to church and we didn't take them to church. Not that we didn't want to. We wish there was a church nearby that stood upon old fashion principles of racial integrity, but there weren't any and so we felt it was better to keep them at home than to place them before the teaching of those who were too weak to proclaim the racial truths of the Bible.

If there had been a local Christian Identity Church, we would have taken them. But there was not and so we did not.

Later, of course, we gathered a few friends and began holding our own church services.

The reason you should not send your kids to your local church is because by doing so you are sending the message to your children that you approve of the teaching they are going to receive.

Unfortunately, most people make the same mistake with their preachers as they do with their politicians. There are crooked congressmen but my congressman is honest. There are bad preachers but my preacher is a good preacher.

AN OLD FASHION PREACHER?

A few years ago I knew this couple who went to a small country church. They told me their preacher was the old fashion kind and did not believe in interracial marriage. It was a small church with a nice White congregation and a weekly attendance between 150 and 200. They said they knew the preacher well and there was no doubt that he was dead-set against race-mixing.

However, a few months later on a Sunday morning, a White girl, a regular attendee at church brought her black boyfriend, which she had met at her school's Christian Bible club.

The couple confronted the preacher who said, that though he was personally against interracial marriage, it wasn't his job to get involved in such matters and that his only duty as a minister was to teach the Gospel.

Of course such a statement is ridiculous. Since when is a Christian minister not to teach moral principle?

Does your preacher have a backbone? Does the preacher or Sunday school teacher of the church your kids attend have a backbone?

HERE IS A TEST YOU CAN GIVE YOUR PREACHER

Ask him if he believes race-mixing is a sin. If he says "No" then get out of that church - fast! *RUN!*

Stop going to that church immediately! And by all means don't let him get his hands on your kids.

You have to be vigilant!

If he says yes, race-mixing is a sin! Then you need to find out if he is sincere or if he is just telling you that because he thinks it is what you want to hear.

Ask him to preach a sermon next Sunday on the sin of race-mixing. I have known many who have done this with their preachers and they have, every one, back-peddled so quickly that hurricane Katrina looked like a summer breeze.

So ask him to preach a sermon on the sin of race-mixing. If he will, then great! But I will lay odds that he will cower before your mere suggestion. If he refuses, (I don't care what kind of excuse he gives or how "nice" he is); ask yourself, *"Why am I going to this church?"* The man is a liar and a coward.

That may sound a little harsh, but what else can you call a preacher who says he is against race-mixing but is afraid to speak out against it? He is more concerned about his standing in the community than he is about teaching our children.

By all means do not attend his church any longer. Do not allow your children to attend! And shame on you if you give even a nickel to the collection plate. Why would you want to finance those who hate the ideals you claim to believe? I don't care how "nice" he is or how many times he gives the altar call.

48

Do not assume that because your child is little he or she is not subject to anti-White propaganda. Children as little as 3 or 4 years old are being taught to sing:

Jesus loves the little children.
All the children of the world.
Red and yellow, black and white.
They are precious in his sight.
Jesus loves the little children of the world.

If your child comes home from Sunday school humming or singing this song then the process to steal him or her away from you has already begun.

It is not an innocent Sunday school song, *but a termite eating at your child's moral foundation.*

Talk to your child and if they are familiar with this song then it's time for the red flag to start waving in your head.

A few years ago, a Southern Baptist Church in Dallas had a sign posted on their church buses which read *"Jesus saves us from racism."* Your church may not so boldly proclaim its commitment to the New Age cult of tolerance, but there are other subtle deceptions and you must be vigilant.

In 1973, the president of the NEA (National Education Association), Catherine Barrett, wrote in the February edition of The Saturday Review of Education, her thoughts on the future of education. According to Barrett,

> *"Dramatic changes in the way we will raise our children in the year 2000 are indicated, particularly in the terms of schooling. We will need to recognize that the so-called basic skills, which currently represent nearly the total effort in elementary schools, will be taught in one-quarter of the present school day. When this happens, and it's near, the teacher can rise to his true calling. More than a dispenser of information, the teacher will be a conveyer of values, a philosopher. We will be **agents of change**."*

These **agents of change** now dominate our schools and churches, often and usually unbeknown to parents. These **agents of change** are also active within our churches. In the May 15th, 2005 edition of PE (Pentecostal Evangel) published by the Assemblies of God, they reveal their proactive commitment to create multi-racial churches. In a two page article titled *AG Multicultural Churches Show Fast, Large Growth*, the author boasts of the change taking place within the church. These tremendous changes have increased the number of churches where no one race is a majority.

Scott Temple, director of Intercultural Ministries for the Assemblies of God says, *"We need to stress planting and growing intercultural churches."* The balance of the article features five interracial churches and the growth they are experiencing. All five featured churches are pastored by a man involved in a mixed "marriage."

The Assemblies of God and racially mixed churches of other denominations are forming the foundation of the One World church much like the Tower of Babel 4,000 years ago. The New Age cult is powerfully deceptive and Christians, because of the agents of change, are easily led down its path.

The purpose of this New Age cult is to bring about a religion of tolerance. This religion of tolerance, whether it is tolerance for miscegenation or tolerance for sodomy, is targeting your children. It is slow - it is methodical - and it is succeeding! Teach your children well!

How to Identify
A One World Church

Most Christian people who are looking at what they call the "end times" are of the opinion that the One World Church is going to be an "anti-Christian" church which they, of course, would never join. However, I think we can easily see that this church is powerfully deceptive and while having the appearance of being Christian, it embraces all who willingly abandon natural laws governing race and gender.

It is also important to understand that the **One World** aspect of this church does not mean a centralized power or location, but only that there is universal acceptance of tolerance.

Because Christian people are being told they must be tolerant like Jesus, they are easy victims.

Though I hate to say it, most churches have entered the Judeo-Christian church world. There are, of course, many who have not. But the takeover of the Christian church and its slow metamorphosis into Judeo-Christianity has sealed the fate of the great majority of previously Christian based churches.

Many people who are trapped in Judeo-Christianity are unaware of how they and their children are being prepared for the One World Church.

Jesus Christ when speaking about the last days in Matthew 24 warns His followers to beware that they do not become deceived by false Christs (Christians?).

Judeo-Christianity is the gateway to the One World Church and because those of the rebellion come as angels (teachers) of light they are able to deceive many.

"And no marvel; for Satan himself is transformed into on angel of light. Therefore it is no great thing if

51

his ministers also be transformed as the ministers of righteousness; whose end shall be according to their works."

2 Corinthians 11:14-15

Spotting a Judeo-Christian church is actually quite easy. However not all Judeo-Christian churches are the same. Some are quite repugnant while others appear rather good. Here are the things to look for.

1) A complete and total commitment to the false State of Israel.
2) Support missionaries or missionary programs to Asia, Africa or South America.
3) Have church bus routes which bring "minority" children from the inner city to your church.
4) Will have non-White teachers, superintendents, etc.
5) Will invite non-White speakers or entertainers to "minister" to your church.
6) Will have programs honoring Martin Luther King's birthday or to celebrate Black History Month.
7) Will have non-Whites in regular attendance at church.
8) Will promote through sermons, Sunday school manuals or activities the teaching of tolerance.
9) The preacher may share in multi-religious conferences or programs with Jewish rabbis, Muslim clerics, etc.
10) The preacher may tell you that he is against integration but will never say so from the pulpit.
11) Sunday school lessons for children will have pictures of White, Asian, Mexican, and Black children in an integrated setting.
12) Children are being taught to sing the *"Jesus loves the little children, all the children of the world . . ."* song.

If you can identify any of the above characteristics of Judeo-Christianity (One World Church) in your church, then the leadership of your church (perhaps ignorantly - that's what being deceived means) is creating the pathway for the One World Church and is aiding the satanic rebellion against God.

Remember, friends or family members trapped in the cult of Judeo-Christianity need your prayers. It's the old bait and switch scheme. People who are lost in sin come to Christ for healing of their lives and the salvation of their souls. But the switch is made by the agents of the rebellion and soon they are trapped in the occult and the New Age Movement of Racial Brotherhood, Racial Reconciliation and coming down the path are our wonderful Christian gay brothers and sisters.

The days of Noah and Lot are upon us!

Made in the USA
Monee, IL
02 January 2024

50999897R00031